MILLBROOK ARTS LIBRARY

RATTLES, BELLS, AND CHIMING BARS

by Karen Foster

The Millbrook Press
Brookfield, Connecticut

Copyright © 1992 Merlion Publishing Ltd
First published in the United States in 1992 by
The Millbrook Press Inc.
2 Old New Milford Road
Brookfield, Connecticut 06804

Consultant: Denys Darlow F.R.C.M., F.L.C.M.
Designer: Tracy Carrington

Printed in the United States by Worzalla.

Library of Congress Cataloging-in-Publication Data
Foster, Karen.
    Rattles, bells, and chiming bars / by Karen Foster.
        p.   cm − (Millbrook arts library)
    Includes glossary and index.
    Summary: Traces the development of percussion instruments
through various cultures, discussing jingles, rattles, gongs and drums.
Includes projects for making instruments.
    ISBN 1-56294-284-O
    1. Percussion instruments–Juvenile literature. 2. Musical meter and
rhythm–Juvenile literature. [1. Percussion instruments.
2. Musical instruments.] I. Title. II. Series.
ML1030.P67 1992
786.8'219–dc20
                                        92-5163
                                           CIP
                                        AC MN

Cover photography by Mike Stannard.

Artwork on pages 24–25, 33 and 36 by Jeremy
Gower; page 40 by Kevin Kimber; pages 4, 7, 13,
15, 18, 26, 29, 35, 37 and 41 by Andrew Midgeley.

Models on pages 5, 17 and 36 by Kate Davies.

Photographs on pages 5, 7, 8, 9, 10–11, 12–13,
14–15, 16, 17, 19, 24–25, 29, 30–31, 34–35, 36
and 39 by Mike Stannard and pages 42-43 by
Toussain Clarke.

CONTENTS

4

Stamping rhythms

A group of Fijian musicians using stamping sticks

When you stamp your foot on the ground you make a single sound. But when you stamp both feet or bang two stones together and then do it again – and again – you start to build a repetitive pattern of sounds. This pattern is called a rhythm. Every piece of music needs some kind of rhythm to keep it moving along. And you need an instrument to make that rhythm. When you bang or stamp out a rhythm, you are using your feet as the instrument.

The instruments that are banged, hit together, or shaken to make a rhythm are known as percussion instruments. The word "percussion" means to strike or shake.

Percussion instruments are among the oldest instruments in the world. In fact, we know from looking closely at cave paintings that they were among the only instruments used in prehistoric times.

Fiji. Stamping sticks usually have one closed end that is banged against the ground. The rhythmic sound echoes up into the tube.

Painted tubes

Collect as many tubes as you can to use for your own stamping sticks. You will need to cover one end with tape or cardboard, and leave the other end open. Decorate the tubes with bright colors and interesting patterns. Take the tubes outside and bang them rhythmically on different surfaces. How does the sound change? Join up with a friend and combine your rhythms!

Stamping sticks

Percussion instruments, especially simple ones, are still popular today because they create such a strong beat to dance and sing to. In Australia, the Aborigines beat hollow sticks on the ground to make an echoing, slightly eerie sound. The sticks are called stamping sticks, and they are also played by tribes from tropical islands such as

Clappers and castanets

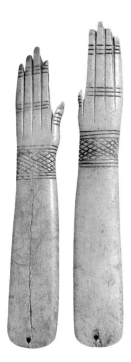

Egyptian ivory hand clappers

When you clap your hands together in time to music, you are using them as a percussion instrument. But your hands are not the only instruments that can clap! Put a stick, a stone, or some other material in each hand. Then bang them together. You've made a hand clapper that you can use to provide a simple background rhythm for many kinds of music.

Ivory hands

Hand clappers have been played for thousands of years by people all over the world. The Ancient Egyptian ivory clappers in the photograph have even been intricately carved in the shape of a pair of hands. Even though these clappers are small – only about 7$\frac{1}{2}$ inches (20 centimeters) long – they can still be used to make a clicking sound.

An Aboriginal musician playing wooden clappers

A pair of clappers made from two smooth bones

Playing with one hand

A pair of clappers can also be played with one hand. Two smooth bones like the ones in the picture, a pair of small stones or sticks, or even a pair of kitchen spoons make simple one-handed clappers. They are held on top of each other in one hand, with the first finger between the two clappers. The thumb controls the top clapper.

The clappers are then banged against the other hand, a knee, or any part of the body, using pressure to make them click together.

Castanets

Castanets are the traditional hand clappers used in Spain. They are made from pairs of small, shell-shaped pieces of wood that are hollowed out and shaped to fit into the palm of the hand. A thin cord links the two pieces and is fitted around the thumb. The player then uses the thumb on one side and the fingers on the other side to click the castanets together. Dancers performing the traditional Spanish flamenco dances often play a pair of castanets with each hand. They stamp their feet to the crisp, cracking rhythm of the castanets, while a guitarist plays exciting flamenco dance music.

A flamenco dancer using castanets

A pair of castanets

Shaking the rattle

that have been hollowed out, dried, and filled with seeds. But rattles can also be made of wood, clay, metal, or leather. Although many of these follow the traditional gourd shape, they can also be stick-shaped or cup-shaped. North American Indians made stick-shaped rattles by stretching leather over a wooden frame and filling it with dried seeds. These rattles were often decorated with beads and feathers.

An ancient rattle

The metal, U-shaped rattle with a handle that is shown in the picture below is a sistrum. When the sistrum is shaken, metal disks threaded onto crossbars rattle against each other to produce a jingling sound. The sistrum was an important instrument in Ancient Egypt. It was played by priests and priestesses during ceremonies to worship the goddess Isis, and it is also known as the Isis clapper.

A rattle is any hollow container filled with small, rattling objects. Rattles make a softer sound than clappers, but they are just as good for providing rhythm. Traditionally, rattles have been made from round vegetables called gourds

A modern pair of maracas

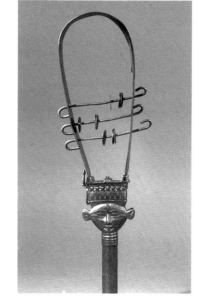

An Egyptian sistrum from 850 B.C.

A modern cabaca

South American rattles

The maracas and the cabaca are two types of rattles played in South America. The maracas are two gourds filled with dried seeds. They can be shaken with one hand or two. Many, such as the ones in the picture, are painted in bright colors. Maracas are probably the best-known rattles in the world. You may have had a chance to play them in a school band. The cabaca is a gourd or a wooden cylinder covered with a mesh of steel beads. The beads rattle together when the instrument is shaken. The picture on the opposite page shows a modern cabaca made from plastic.

Guess what's in the container?

Set up a quiz for your family and friends, using a variety of materials that can rattle in a container. A can with a lid is ideal, because your materials will make a loud sound inside it. Find some small, hard objects like lentils, dried beans, buttons or rice.

Place a handful of one of your materials into the container and put the lid on. Now shake the can rhythmically and ask everyone to identify the objects rattling inside and to name the one they think works best. Keep the material that makes everyone's favorite sound and use your can as a rattle.

The clash of cymbals

These Tibetan musicians are playing cymbals at a New Year ceremony

A cymbal is a round plate usually made from bronze or brass, which is hollowed out in the center. Cymbals are normally played as a pair. No one knows where cymbals originally came from, although it might have been China, India, or the Middle East. Certainly Tibetan monks, like those in the picture, have been using cymbals in their religious ceremonies for thousands of years. Today, cymbals of many shapes and sizes are played in most countries around the world.

Finger cymbals

Finger cymbals are the smallest type of cymbal. They are attached to the middle finger and thumb with loops of string and are clicked together to play a rhythm. Finger cymbals make an ideal instrument to accompany dancing, because the performers can beat their own rhythm while they dance.

A pair of finger cymbals

A pair of orchestral cymbals

Hand-held cymbals

The large cymbals you can see in the center of this page are played with two hands. They are held by a leather strap that is wound around each hand, and they are held vertically at a distance from each other. The player can make a dramatic ringing sound by clashing the two cymbals together, or a softer, swishing sound by brushing them together in an up-and-down movement. At the end of the 1800s, hand-held cymbals were first introduced into western orchestras. You can read more about orchestras on pages 36 and 37.

You can read more about orchestras on pages 36 and 37.

Modern cymbals

Today, large single cymbals are often seen as part of drum kits used by rock bands. You can see a drum kit in this picture. Mechanical cymbals are played by pressing on a foot pedal. This raises the top cymbal and then releases it to come crashing down on the lower one. Since the cymbals are operated by foot, the drummer can play as many fast cymbal clashes as needed and still have both hands free to play the drums.

Cymbal makers

Most of the cymbals produced today are made by an Armenian family firm, named Zildjian, who have been making cymbals since the 1700s. Originally, the Zildjian factory was located in Istanbul, but today it is based in the United States. The firm uses a secret mixture of metals and perfected cymbal making to such a level that it is famous worldwide for instruments that produce a tone that is clear and that vibrates for a long period of time.

A modern drum set

Sounding a gong

A modern gong, part of a western orchestra

Have you ever heard a gong being played? If you have, it was probably a large orchestral gong hanging on a stand, like the one in the picture on the left. Can you imagine what kind of sound an instrument like this makes? A single strike is deep and rich with echoing vibrations that continue for up to a minute.

What is a gong?

A gong is a circular plate made from a mixture of copper and tin. Today's gongs are based on instruments first made in Asia, probably from metal cooking plates. We know that a gong was made in China as early as A.D. 500. Asian gongs play an important part in religious festivals. They have become a sign of wealth. Silver or gold is added to the copper and tin mixture, and the gongs are often beautifully carved and mounted on elaborate frames.

Orchestral gongs are made to play a specific sound, called a note. This means that, unlike the other percussion instruments we have looked at, gongs are tuned until they have the exact note the maker requires. A gong is tuned by changing the thickness of the metal. All gongs are struck, or sounded, with a wooden mallet covered with felt or wool, called a beater. Try wrapping a cloth around a stick to use as your own homemade beater.

Gong chimes

Gong chimes are sets of pot-shaped gongs mounted in wooden racks. They are found mainly in Indonesia. As many as 12 gongs of different sizes rest on cords inside the frame. Each gong is tuned to play a different note.

A khong wong lek from the Bangkok School of Music and Dance in Thailand

A row of gongs from the Philippines, called a kulintangan

There are many different kinds of gong chimes, and their names often depend on the shape of the frame. The row of gong chimes from the Philippines in the picture above are mounted on a straight, low frame. The Javanese bonnang has a similar frame but holds two rows of gongs, not one.

A circular frame

The gong in the picture above is the khong wong lek from Thailand. It has a circular wooden frame that the player sits inside. Can you see the large padded beaters the player uses? They make a soft sound. The khong wong lek and the bonnang are played with great skill in the Indonesian gamelan orchestras, which you can read more about on pages 26–29.

A picture of a decorated Chinese gong

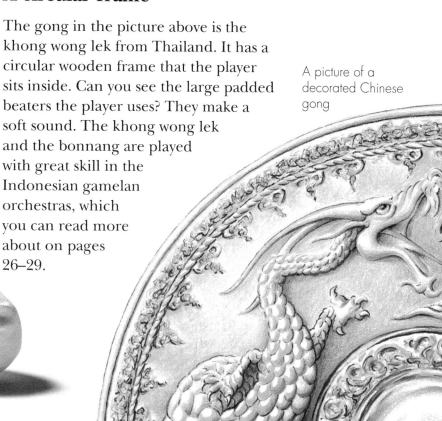

A gong beater

Pots, cans, and bottles

Look around your home and collect as many empty glass bottles as you can find. You will need at least eight – but make sure they are the same size and check that nobody needs them! Arrange them in a row and fill the first one almost full of water. Fill the next bottle with slightly less water, and so on until the last bottle has only a small amount of water in it.

Now find a beater. You can use any kind of stick. Start by tapping the first bottle. What kind of sound does it make? Now tap the last bottle. Does it make a different sound? Tap each bottle in turn to play a scale.

Percussion vessels

Each of your bottles is a musical instrument called a percussion vessel.

By filling each one with a different amount of water, you have created a tuned instrument. People have been playing tuned percussion vessels for thousands of years and, just like you, they originally made their instruments from ordinary household objects. People found out that they could make a lower note by putting more water in their vessels.

The jalaterang

Later, people used china, tin, and glass objects as percussion vessels. The porcelain bowls in this picture make an instrument called a jalaterang, which comes from India. The bowls are filled with different amounts of water and arranged in a semi-circle in front of the player. They are played with thin bamboo sticks to produce beautiful, crystal-clear sounds.

Skilled jalaterang players can produce a quivering note by placing a small wooden spoon into the bowl just after it has been struck. By moving the spoon in and out of the water, they can change the note from a pure one to a quivering one. This note explains the instrument's name – jalaterang means "water waves."

An Indian jalaterang

Making music with a glass

Have you ever heard anyone rubbing their finger around the rim of a drinking glass to make an eerie, high-pitched sound? If you have, you may not think this noise is very musical, but some composers in the 1800s and 1900s thought it made interesting music.

In the 1760s, the American inventor Benjamin Franklin developed a new instrument from the musical glasses. It consisted of 24 glass bowls of different sizes mounted so that their lower rims dipped into a trough full of water. The bowls were turned mechanically so that the rims stayed wet enough to be played with a finger, just like the drinking glasses. Franklin called his instrument the glass harmonica. The famous Austrian composer Wolfgang Amadeus Mozart even wrote a piece of music for Franklin's new instrument.

Benjamin Franklin's glass harmonica

A scraping sound

Look carefully at the objects on this page. Imagine rubbing your fingers over them. What would they feel like? They would probably feel interesting to touch, because they are all ridged or uneven in some way. They all have a textured surface.

How would you use the texture of objects like these to make musical sounds? You might rub the fir cones together to make a dull, knocking noise. You might scrape the shells together to make a scratching noise. Or you might find a stick to rub against both of them to make sharper sounds.

Wood and bone scrapers

All of these objects have been used at some time to make a kind of musical instrument known as a scraper. People have also copied these natural sounds by carving deep ridges into bone, or animal horns. The ridges make a loud,

A modern scraper from Mexico

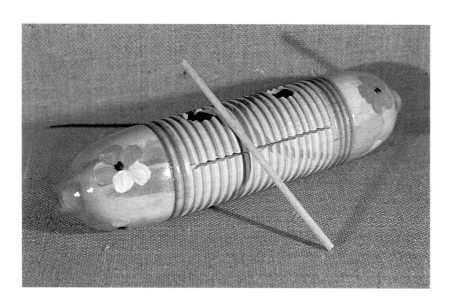

rasping sound when they are rubbed with a stick. Australian Aborigines make scrapers carved in the shapes of animals and play them with a wooden stick.

A modern scraper

The brightly-colored wooden tube in the picture is a modern scraper from Mexico. The ridges are rubbed with a stick to make a clicking sound that provides the rhythm for Latin American dance music. Can you see the slit cut along the length of the tube? This lets out the sound that bounces around, or resonates, inside the tube as it is being scraped. Resonators like this hollow scraper make louder and richer sounds than an ordinary scraper.

Scraper boards

The metal scraper board in the picture below is called a washboard. Washboards were originally designed for holding dirty clothes while they were rubbed with soap, but like many other household objects, the washboard was adopted as a musical instrument. It was used to play a kind of American music popular in the 1950s called skiffle. Skiffle musicians sing fast-beat folksongs and play guitars and other homemade instruments.

Skiffle players usually hold the washboard across one knee. The player scrapes the board with a metal rod or wears metal caps on each finger to make a loud, continuous sound. The washboard in the picture has been specially made so that it can be hung from the musician's neck, which makes it easier to play.

Make a cane scraper

You can make your own scraper from strips of cane. First, ask an adult to help you to cut the cane into lengths of about 7½ inches (20 centimeters). Use some brightly colored string to tie them tightly together in a line. Then use a stick or a pencil to rub over the top of the canes to play a rhythm. If you put your scraper on top of a box or a bowl, the sound will resonate.

A washboard player from a skiffle band

Plucked percussion

A nomadic
Masai tribe

The Masai tribes of Africa are nomadic, which means they move around the country looking for fresh food and water for their cattle. The Masai people make music with an instrument ideally suited to their lifestyle. It is a small set of metal keys called an mbira, pronounced "umbira." It is also known as a sansa or thumb piano. The mbira is small and light enough to be easily packed away and carried when the tribe moves on.

The keys of the mbira are usually made from slivers of bamboo or strips of metal. Each key is fixed to two wooden or metal bridges that are attached to a hollow wood or bamboo block. One end of each key is left free to vibrate when it is plucked with the thumb and fingers. This vibration makes the twanging sound of mbira music.

A South African
mbira

A modern
jew's harp

A thumb piano
from Zimbabwe

Improving the sound

Look at the picture above that shows a kind of modern mbira, called a kalimba. You can see that the keys are exactly like those of the mbira, but the kalimba is played inside a hollow gourd. The gourd acts as a resonator. It makes the sound of the plucked keys louder.

Mouth harps

The Balinese musicians in the picture on the right are playing mouth harps. These instruments have one flexible bamboo or metal key, and the musicians hold them in the mouth to play. Can you think why they do this? It's because the musicians use their mouths as resonators.

You may have seen a modern mouth harp like the one above. This instrument is called a jew's harp. People think that its name comes from the word "jaw," because of the way it is played. The jew's harp is not often heard today, but in the 1920s it was a popular instrument in certain kinds of jazz bands.

Moving your mouth

You can experiment with your mouth as a resonator by using a rubber band stretched between your thumb and first finger. Put the band up to your mouth and twang it with the fingers of your other hand. As you do so, move your mouth to make different shapes with your lips. How does this affect the sound you make? Experiment with your mouth movements until you get the best sound.

Mouth harp players
from the Bing Gong
Orchestra in Bali

Stone chimes

A Chinese
pien ch'ing

"When I smite my musical stone – be it gently or strong,
Then do the fiercest hearts leap for joy, and the chiefs do agree among themselves."

This verse was written in about 2300 B.C. by a musician named Konei. Konei was court musician to the Chinese Emperor Yao. His verse describes the beautiful music he played on an instrument called a pien ch'ing. Pien ch'ings, like the one in the picture, are formed from two rows of L-shaped

stones that are hung from a carved wooden frame. The stones are hung in order of size to make a scale or several scales, the smaller stones making the higher sounds.

Pien ch'ings are still played in China today. You may not think that stones could produce any sound other than a dull thud. But Konei's verse tells you how musical the stones can be if they are played well. They are struck with a soft beater to produce clear, chiming notes.

Volcanic stones

Stone chimes, such as the pien ch'ing, are called lithophones. The stones used to make lithophones are not ordinary stones. Scientists believe that the stones have been affected by volcanic eruptions. They think that the enormous heat from a volcano changes the structure of some kinds of stones. When the stones cool down again, they produce a clear, ringing sound when they are struck. This sound is quite unlike the sound made by any other stone. People may have discovered the musical sound made by these stones by using them as cutting boards or anvils.

English lithophones

Special volcanic stones were found in the Lake District, a hilly area of England, in the early 1900s. Several local people made lithophones by cutting the stones into slabs and arranging them according to size on a wooden frame. The picture above shows one of these simple lithophones.

The huge lithophone below comes from the same part of England and was made at the same time, but you can see that it is a much more complicated instrument. It was made by members of the Richardson family, who also became expert at playing it.

A simple stone lithophone from Keswick, England

The Richardson lithophone from Keswick, England

Chiming bars

A gourd xylophone
from Sierra Leone

Chimes made from wood and metal are more familiar than the stone lithophones. Usually, the wood or metal is cut into bars of different sizes and placed on a frame. Wooden chiming bars are called xylophones, and metal chiming bars are called metallophones.

Metallophones and xylophones are tuned instruments. Each bar is cut to an exact length and thickness to produce the chosen note accurately. The smallest bars play the highest notes in the scale, and the largest bars play the lowest ones. The bars are fixed to the frame in order of size so that the notes build on each other in scales. You can read more about this on pages 24 and 25.

Improving the sound

The large xylophone in the picture above comes from Africa. Can you see the gourds hanging underneath each wooden bar? The largest gourd contains the most air. It is hung beneath the largest and lowest-sounding bar.

The gourds are resonators. The air inside each one strengthens the sound of the note made by the bar above it. Sometimes the gourds have a hole at their base. These holes are covered with the thin web-like material that spiders spin to cover their eggs. When the note is played, this soft material vibrates, adding an interesting buzzing sound to the note.

Marimbas

The spectacular xylophone in the picture above is called a marimba. It comes from Central America. The wooden tubes hanging down underneath it are carved resonators. The marimba is much larger than most xylophones. As you can see, several musicians play it at the same time.

Like other xylophones, it is struck with soft-ended mallets to produce a rich, melodic sound.

Metallophones

Metallophones look similar to xylophones, but they have bars made of copper or steel instead of wood. They are particularly important instruments in the Far East. The beautifully carved metallophone below is called a saron. The carved wooden box is a resonator. In Indonesia, sarons are used to play the main tune, or melody, in special bands called gamelan orchestras. You can read more about these on pages 26–29.

There is another metallophone which is played in the gamelan orchestra. It is called a gender. Unlike the saron, it has a separate bamboo resonator for each bar. The gender produces a softer, more muted sound, that adds to the melody played by the saron.

A marimba band from Guatemala

A saron from Indonesia

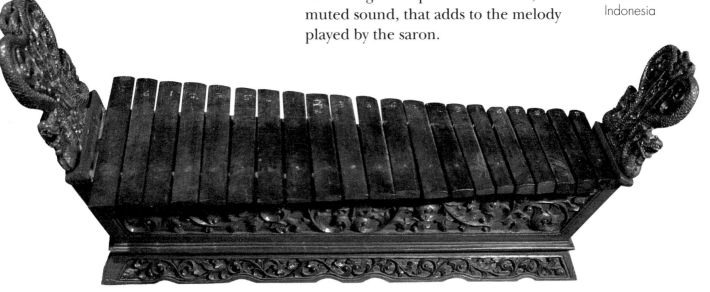

Playing the orchestral chiming bars

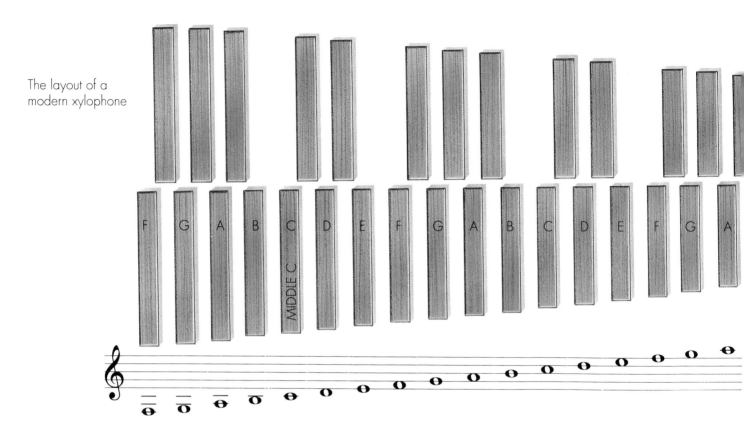

The layout of a modern xylophone

F G A B C (MIDDLE C) D E F G A B C D E F G A

All modern western orchestras include a group of percussion instruments, that is known as the percussion section. Chiming bars are an important part of this section. The orchestral xylophone and marimba are just modern versions of the chiming bars we have already looked at. The percussion section also usually includes a metallophone called a glockenspiel.

You play these three instruments with sticks covered at one end with rubber, wood, or plastic. You have to use a light touch to make sure your stick bounces quickly off the bar as you strike it. If you let your stick linger on the bar, the note will be muffled rather than clear and true.

Holding your sticks

The chiming bars are played by hitting the bars with the right and left hand alternately. You hold each stick between your thumb and index finger, with your palm pointing downward. You can extend the forefinger to improve the control.

Holding one stick

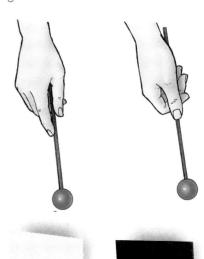

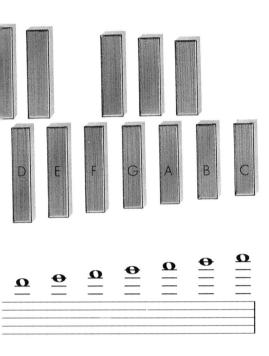

D E F G A B C

Playing the xylophone

The Scottish percussionist, Evelyn Glennie, playing the xylophone

To find out how to play the chiming bars, we can look in detail at the xylophone. The diagram on the left shows how the bars are laid out according to their size. Each bar plays one note. Each note is named after one of the first seven letters of the alphabet: A, B, C, D, E, F, and G. Western music is based on a scale of eight notes, which is called an octave. Each octave starts and ends with a note of the same name. One simple octave starts with the note C. Find a C on the diagram. Then find the C that is eight notes, or an octave, higher. This C sounds higher than middle C. We say it has higher pitch.

The xylophone's scales go from F through C. Count the notes. You will see that there are three and a half octaves on the bottom set of bars. All these notes are the main notes. The top set of bars are notes that fall between the main notes. The xylophone player has to watch the instrument and the conductor and read the music – and all of these at the same time!

Look at the photograph of the talented Scottish percussionist Evelyn Glennie on this page. She is using four sticks, two in each hand, to play a xylophone. To hold two sticks in one hand, cross the sticks under your palm with the stick pointing inward on top. Use your thumb and forefinger to control the movement of the sticks.

Holding two sticks

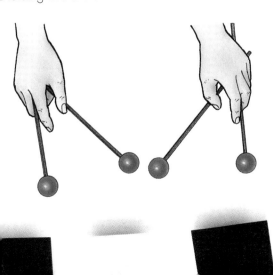

The gamelan orchestra

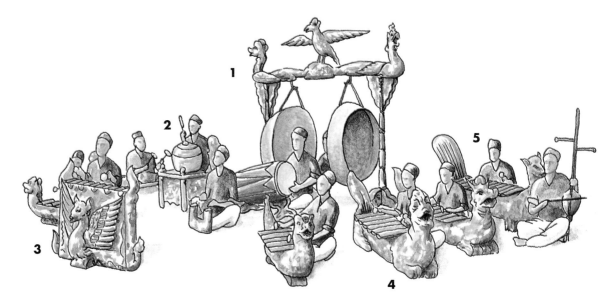

The layout of an average gamelan orchestra

1. gong ageng
2. bonnang
3. gender
4. saron
5. gambang kayu

The picture on the opposite page shows a group of musicians, most of whom are playing percussion instruments. This is a gamelan orchestra, and it is a common sight in Indonesia. Most villages have their own orchestra, that plays a central role in village life. The local orchestra, its instruments, and its music are the pride of every community.

The instruments

A gamelan orchestra can consist of up to 40 instruments, all of which are usually made from bronze. They can be made from bamboo, but this gives a poorer-quality sound. Because the instruments are always made by a local specialist, each orchestra has a different sound.

The arrangement of the instruments is important. There are nine basic types of instruments in the larger gamelans, and their position on the stage follows a set pattern. You can see this pattern in the picture above. You will notice that there can be several instruments of each type in one orchestra.

The spirit of the orchestra

The most important instrument is the main gong, or gong ageng. It hangs from a wooden frame and produces a deep, ringing sound when struck. Many believe that the gong ageng is the home of the spirit of the orchestra, and people will often pay to get some of the water the instrument has been washed in because they believe it has special powers. Other gongs in the orchestra are called the khong wong lek and the bonnang. You have already read about these on page 13.

Melodic chiming bars

Xylophones and metallophones are also important gamelan instruments. The main tune, or melody, is played on a metallophone called a saron, while another metallophone, the gender, supports the melody. You have read about these instruments on page 23. The gamelan orchestra also usually contains a xylophone which is called a gambang kayu.

A gamelan orchestra playing at a festival in Bali

Gamelan music

An Indonesian puppet show

Gamelan music is built around a scale of five notes that is often used in Eastern music. It is called a pentatonic scale. All the instruments in the gamelan orchestra are tuned to two different pitches, called slendro and pelog. Many orchestras have two sets of all the instruments, one for each pitch. The players switch between the two pitches, but never mix them. Each slendro instrument is placed at a right angle to its pelog partner.

The musicians play from memory. They learn the basic tunes by heart and then add to them as they feel like it, a technique that we call improvisation. The music falls into sections, called gongans, each of which finishes with a stroke on the gong ageng. There is a pause, and then the next gongan begins. The musicians are usually so skilled that they amaze their audiences with their playing.

Spiritual music

The gamelan orchestra plays an important part in spiritual life. Its music accompanies religious ceremonies and important events such as weddings. This means that the orchestra itself has a special spiritual meaning for local people. There are many rituals associated with the orchestra. For example, each instrument is thought to have its own character. A musician will never step over an instrument because it would be disrespectful to do so.

Music for entertainment

The gamelan is also an important part of the most exciting form of entertainment in Indonesia – puppet shows. The puppets are made of leather, wood, and cloth and are controlled with bamboo sticks. They are moved behind a screen so that lamps throw their shadows onto the screen, just as in the picture at the top of this page. Most performances start in the late evening and continue until dawn.

During a performance, the orchestra is controlled by one person, called the dalang, who is also the puppeteer and narrator. The dalang skillfully moves beautifully decorated puppets, like the ones in the picture below, while gamelan music plays.

Two Indonesian puppets

Bells for dancing

An Indian picture, painted in 1850, called *Three Musicians and a Dancing Girl*

The Indian dancer stands completely still. She bends her knees and her legs point outward from her body. Then she slowly raises one hand and slightly turns one ankle as she begins to dance. She stamps her foot – first her heel and then her toes. She twists her hands and fingers. Her head turns from side to side, and her eyes stare.

Traditional Indian dances are very powerful in their effect. It is the sounds the dancer makes that really create the drama. Each time she moves her neck, her wrists, or her ankles, small bells ring. These tiny bells are called jingles. They are worn by dancers so that the sound they make draws attention to every movement, no matter how small it is.

Pellet bells

On its own, one of these small bells would make very little noise, so several are always grouped together to increase the effect. Jingles are also called pellet bells because they have a small pellet inside them. The pellet rattles around against the metal case to make the bell sound.

A jingle from Spain

Morris dancing

In England, there is a type of folk dancing called Morris dancing. Morris dancing is a celebration of good fortune that takes place at special times of the year, such as after the harvest. The dancers, dressed in white and decorated with brightly colored ribbons, wear jingles on ribbons around each knee. Some of the dancers carry sticks covered with bells to shake. As they jump and shout, the bells add to the excitement of this happy dance.

Because jingles are worn by dancers, they are often thought of as jewelry rather than as musical instruments. Jingles became more and more elaborate and were often made of gold or silver, like the Spanish jingle above.

Shells and nuts

Jingles can be made from many kinds of materials. People have used shells and nuts threaded onto thongs as simple instruments for thousands of years. You can make your own jingle jewelry from beads, shells, or pasta shapes threaded onto string.

Cut your strings into different lengths before you thread on your chosen jingles. Then you can knot them around your ankles or wrists like an Indian dancer, or around your knees like a Morris dancer.

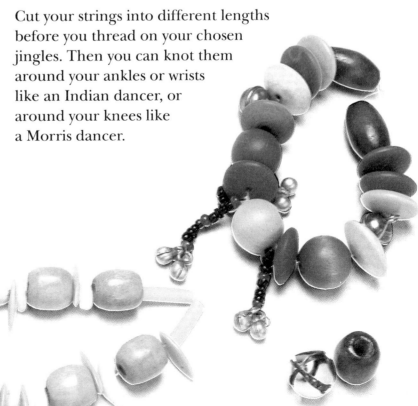

Striking the bell

The enormous Russian bell in the picture below is the heaviest bell in the world. It is called the Czar Kolokol bell, and it weighs nearly 200 tons. It was made in 1735, but it was too heavy to be used. It now stands on a large platform in the Kremlin in Moscow. A fragment of the huge bell has broken away, and even this piece weighs about 11 tons!

Not all bells are as large as the Kolokol bell, but many are much older. Metal bells dating from 1000 B.C. have been found in the Middle East, in Iran. People in many countries have used the sound made by wooden or metal bells to frighten away enemies and evil spirits. Bells are often used in religious ceremonies and as charms to bring people good fortune.

A picture of the huge Russian Kolokol bell

A Japanese temple bell

Sounding a bell

All bells need an instrument to strike, or sound, them. They must be struck on the rim, where the metal is thickest, to produce the loudest sound. Each bell makes a different musical note. The larger the bell is, the lower the note. A bell can be struck from the inside or the outside, and the striker can be attached to the bell or can be separate from it.

Temple bells

The picture on the right shows a large Japanese temple bell. It is struck on the outside with a wooden beam pulled by a rope. Bells like this are usually housed in a special building within the grounds of the temple and are rung to call people to prayer.

Clapper bells

Most bells are sounded by an instrument that is attached to the inside of the bell. This is called a clapper. Clappers can be made of several different materials, such as bone or shell, but most are forged from metal. Clappers can also be round or square in shape.

Change ringing

In Europe, bell towers are a feature of many churches. The bells are hung high up in the tower and rung in groups of five or more. This is called change ringing, and it is a complicated skill that takes a long time to learn. These pictures show you how it is done.

Each bell is mounted on a wooden wheel, which can be moved by pulling the rope attached to it. Each bell ringer pulls his or her rope down, and the bell swings up on its wheel. He or she pulls down again, and the bell swings down, ringing as it falls. Each bell has a different note and must be rung at just the right time so that the result is an evenly spaced set of sounds, called a peal. As you can imagine, it is crucial that each bell ringer pull down at precisely the right second. This is especially important when the peal gives way to a tune.

1. The bell is in its resting position

2. A series of gentle pulls swings the bell upside down. A brake, or stay, stops it from swinging over the top

3. A sharp pull on the rope swings the bell down. It strikes and then continues up again

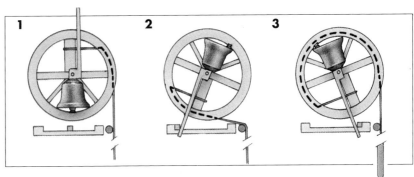

Playing the hand bells

A set of 13 English
hand bells

Hand bells are the same shape as the larger church bells, but are small enough to be held in the hand with a leather strap. The bells are made of a special metal called bronze. Inside each bell there is a clapper to hit the sides and create the sound. The clapper is a metal rod with hard leather pads on the end. Below the hand strap there is a leather collar. This prevents the bell from being touched as it rings, since this would spoil the tone.

Tibetan monks
playing hand bells
during a religious
ceremony

Carrying a bell

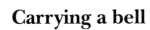

Hand-held bells have been used throughout the ages to send signals. The sound of a hand bell would announce that the bell ringer had an important message. Messengers would walk the streets ringing a hand bell and shouting news to people walking by. This still happens on special occasions in some European countries, where the messengers are called town criers.

Ringing for pleasure

Today, some people play hand bells just for fun or to entertain others. They hold one bell in each hand and follow written music. The bells are so finely tuned and so light to control that all kinds of music can be played on them.

Each hand bell produces a different musical note, so when a group of eight or more bells ring together, quite complicated music can be played on them. The smaller the hand bell, the higher the pitch of the musical note. The deeper-sounding hand bells are sometimes so large that they have to be played resting on a table.

Hand bells are popular instruments in schools. Many schools have groups of hand bell players, who perform at assemblies and at local events.

A single English hand bell

Orchestral percussion

Look at this diagram of a western orchestra. You can see that each set of instruments has its own place on the stage. Can you see the percussion section? It is right at the back, in the center. In a large orchestra, there may be three or four percussionists playing a variety of instruments.

Every percussion section has a basic selection of those instruments that are normally required by composers. They are the timpani (sometimes called the kettledrums), the snare drum, the bass drum, the gong, the cymbals, the xylophone, and the glockenspiel.

The composer decides

Some pieces of music are written to include other percussion instruments, too. Some music calls for percussion instruments such as the mbira, tubular bells, triangle, and castanets. At some performances, the percussion section can contain as many as 80 instruments!

The triangle

You already know about most of the instruments in the percussion section, but you haven't yet read about the triangle or the tubular bells. You can see from the picture below that a triangle is a thin steel bar bent into the shape of a triangle. One corner is left open. It is played by tapping the outside of the bars with a steel beater to produce a high, pure sound that can be used to resemble bells.

A triangle and beater

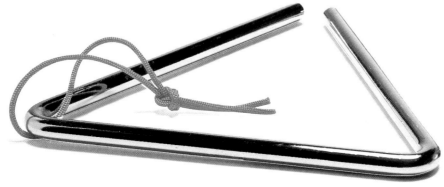

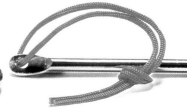

A percussionist plays the orchestral tubular bells

The British composer Benjamin Britten

Tubular bells

Tubular bells are formed by hanging two rows of different-length steel tubes from a frame in order of size. The largest tube produces the lowest sound. Can you see how they are played by looking at the picture on the right? They are struck at the top with a mallet covered with leather or felt. Listen to tubular bells in the opera called *The Turn of the Screw,* by the British composer Benjamin Britten.

Playing orchestral percussion

To be a successful percussionist you must be able to play all the instruments in the percussion section. This requires many different skills, and may take years to learn. The famous British percussionist James Blades has achieved this, and he is also well known for making and collecting percussion instruments. You could follow his example by making some of the instruments in this book and then learning to play them.

Wind chimes and the musical saw

A painting of Richard Wagner by the German artist Gemaelde von Schweninsky

This is a painting of the German composer Richard Wagner. Wagner is probably best known for his series of four operas called *The Ring of the Nibelung*. In one of the operas, *The Rhine Gold*, Wagner wrote a scene that uses an anvil as a percussion instrument.

The scene shows Wotan, the chief of the gods, arriving at a cave belonging to a band of dwarfs. The music grows gloomy to reflect the eerie mood of the cave. Slowly the orchestral music dies down, until only one dramatic sound can be heard. It is a slow tapping of metal on metal as one of the dwarfs works at his anvil. The curtain lowers as the tapping echoes around the stage, and the scene ends as the sound dies away.

The anvil is just one of several unusual percussion instruments that composers like Wagner have used to great effect. The percussionist does not use a real anvil to achieve the dramatic sound Wagner's opera demands. Instead, an orchestral anvil made from two or more steel bars is used.

The musical saw

The musical saw is another unusual percussion instrument. It is based on the ordinary carpenter's saw, but it does not have teeth. The blade is held between the player's knees and bent into an S shape. It is played with a cello bow to produce a ghostly, squeaking sound. As you can guess, it is a difficult instrument to play!

An American musical saw player

Tinkling in the wind

Wind chimes create the completely opposite effect from those of the anvil and the musical saw. They are made of small pieces of shell, glass, metal, or wood, suspended from cords. Wind chimes were originally made in the Far East and hung in temples, where the wind moved them naturally to create a pleasing tinkling sound. They are not often used in the orchestra, but when they are, they are moved by hand.

Make your own wind chimes

First, cut out a circle of thick cardboard, about 4 inches (10 centimeters) in diameter. Make a circle of eight small holes around the edge and one hole in the center of the circle. Cut nine strings of different lengths, and thread one through each hole. Make knots in the top to hold them in place. Now ask an adult to cut some pieces of bamboo or cane for you. Thread one onto each piece of string and make a knot in the end. Hang up your chimes, and let the wind move the wood together. Try using stones to make a different sound.

A steel band from
Barbados

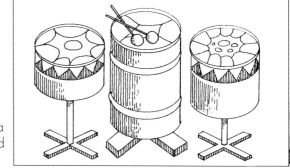

A tenor pan, a
guitar pan and
a bass pan

Carnival music

You are in a hot, sunny country walking through a busy market, full of bright colors and exotic smells. What kind of music would you like to be listening to? Would it be slow, sad music? No, you would probably want to hear music with a rhythm to match your cheerful mood.

There is one instrument that would produce just the right kind of lively music for these occasions. It is called the steel drum, or pan, and it comes from Trinidad in the West Indies. Carnivals are important events there, and people have always joined in the joyful celebrations by banging out a lively rhythm on anything they could find, from cookie tins to trash cans.

Eventually, someone found that steel oil drums made a rich, musical sound and steel pans are still made from oil drums today.

Different notes

The first steel pan players found they could play different notes by making different-sized bulges in the surface of the pan. Then they cut the main body of the drum to different sizes and found that this gave the notes different tones. You can find out how a steel pan is made by turning to pages 42 and 43.

The steel band

The large picture on the opposite page shows you what a steel band looks like when it is made up of several different-sized steel pans. There are three sections in a steel band. You can see the shape of the pans in each section in the diagram. The smallest pan is called the tenor pan. It produces the highest note and is used to play the main tune, which we call the melody. The guitar pan is the middle-sized pan. It is used to play the rhythm. The bass pan is the largest pan, and it has the deepest notes. It is used to play another, complementary rhythm.

Steel bands can have many members, all playing different variations of the three main kinds of pan. A good steel band can play almost any kind of music, from rock music, reggae and calypso to classical music.

Making a steel pan

Many steel pan players make their own instruments so that they can be sure that the pan they play has exactly the sound they want. Making a steel pan is a complicated job, with nine main stages.

First, a drum is chosen. If you look back to pages 36 and 37, you will see that there are three types of steel pan. Here, a drum with the right thickness of metal to make a tenor pan is selected.

Now the end of the oil drum is pounded with a heavy leather mallet. It must be pounded into a smooth curve about $7\frac{1}{2}$ inches (20 centimeters) deep. This process is called sinking the pan.

Sinking the pan

Tracing the notes

Patterns of the notes are traced onto the sunken shape with chalk. The tenor pan has 28 notes, and these have to be marked in a precise way.

Now the shape of each note must be punched into the metal. You can see how this is done using a punch and a hammer to make lots of indentations.

Punching in the notes

Cutting the pan

Heating the metal

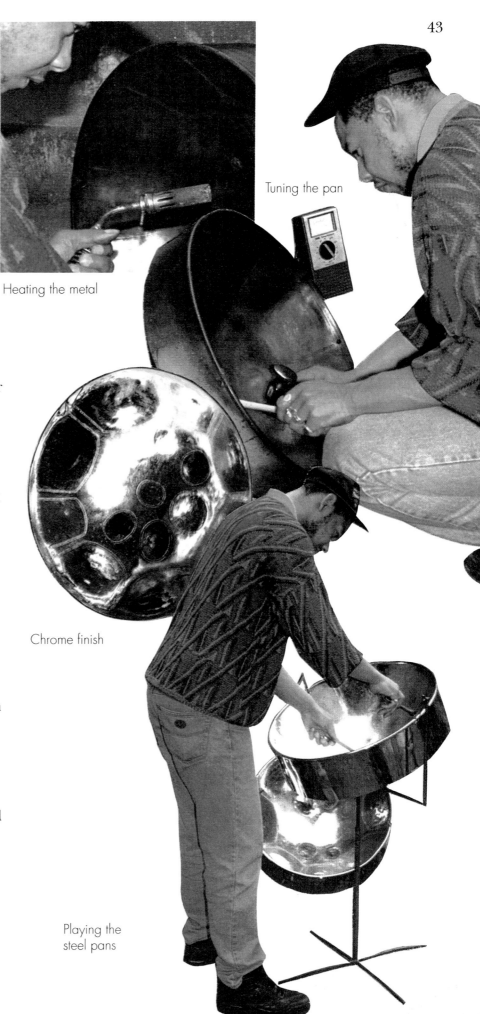

Tuning the pan

Chrome finish

Playing the
steel pans

The main part of the barrel is now cut to the right size, using a metal cutter. The shorter the pan, the higher the range of notes it will produce. The tenor pan is cut to about $7\frac{1}{2}$ inches (20 centimeters) deep.

Now the surface metal of the pan has to be heated up quickly. Sometimes the whole pan is plunged into a bonfire, but here a blowtorch is being used. Once the metal cools down again, it is much softer and easier to mold.

Now comes the most important stage – tuning. The drum maker taps out the standard note with a rubber-tipped beater. Then he taps the soft metal over and over again on the same spot, using gentle strokes until the sound of the note begins to change. He tunes the pan by ear, checking each note with a mechanical tuner to make sure it is accurate.

He does the same on the marked-out places of each of the 28 notes positioned around the pan. Now the pan is sent away to a factory where it is dipped in a liquid metal called chrome. This gives the finished pan its bright, shiny look.

Finally, the pan is fixed to its stand. At last it is ready to play.

GLOSSARY OF INSTRUMENTS

anvil: a percussion instrument consisting of steel bars that are hit with a metal striker.

bell: a hollow metal instrument struck either from inside by a clapper or from outside by a striker.

bonnang: Javanese gong chimes with two rows of gongs in a straight, low frame.

cabaca: a gourd covered with a mesh of beads that rattle when shaken.

castanets: a Spanish instrument consisting of two shell-shaped pieces of wood that are clicked together.

chiming bars: a set of bars of different length and thickness, beaten with small hammers.

clappers: two pieces of the same material that are struck together.

cymbals: dishes of bronze or brass with leather handles. They can be clashed together as a pair, or struck individually with a drumstick.

finger cymbals: small cymbals that are played with the finger and thumb.

gambang kayu: a xylophone played in a gamelan orchestra.

gamelan: an Indonesian orchestra consisting of percussion instruments.

gender: a kind of metallophone played in a gamelan orchestra.

glass harmonica: a set of glasses played by rubbing a moistened finger round the rim of the glass.

glockenspiel: a set of tuned metal bars played with small hammers.

gong: a large metal plate hung on a frame and hit with a mallet.

gong ageng: a gong, hung on a wooden frame, played in a gamelan orchestra.

gong chimes: a set of pot-shaped gongs mounted in wooden racks.

hand bells: a set of small tuned bells that are played by hand.

jalaterang: a set of percussion vessels from India, played with thin bamboo sticks.

jew's harp: a mouth harp with one flexible key made from bamboo or metal.

jingle: a small bell or rattling object attached to a stick or frame and shaken, or worn by a dancer.

kalimba: an mbira played inside a hollow gourd.

khong wong lek: a set of Thai gongs set in a circular wooden frame.

kulintangan: a row of gongs from the Philippines.

lithophone: a set of stones of different sizes that produce a clear sound when struck.

maracas: a pair of gourds filled with dried seeds.

marimba: a Central American xylophone with tubular resonators.

mbira: a set of metal strips fixed to a wood block. The mbira is also known as the sansa or thumb piano.

metallophone: a set of tuned chiming bars made of metal.

mouth harp: an instrument with one flexible key made from bamboo or metal, played in the mouth.

musical saw: a saw that is held between the player's knees, bent over, and played with a cello bow.

pellet bell: a small bell with a rattling pellet inside.

percussion instrument: an instrument that is hit or shaken.

percussion vessel: a container with water inside, which is struck with sticks or hands.

pien ch'ing: a set of two rows of L-shaped stones of different size, struck with a soft beater.

rattle: a hollow container filled with small objects which rattle when shaken.

saron: an Indonesian metallophone played in a gamelan orchestra.

scraper: a rough or ridged object that is rubbed with a rod or with the fingers.

sistrum: a U-shaped rattle with metal discs threaded onto crossbars.

stamping stick: a hollow tube, closed at one end, that is banged against the ground.

steel pan: a tuned percussion instrument made from an oil drum.

triangle: a metal bar in a three-cornered shape, struck with a steel beater.

tubular bells: a tuned set of metal tubes hung from a frame. They are played with a mallet or drumsticks.

washboard: a scraper originally used for washing clothes.

wind chimes: small pieces of shell, glass, metal or wood hung from strings. They jingle together in the wind.

xylophone: a set of tuned wooden blocks laid out like a keyboard and hit with a mallet.

INDEX

ACKNOWLEDGMENTS

The publishers would like to thank the following for permission to reproduce these photographs:

Ace Photo Library for steel band from Barbados (page 40). Axel Poignant Archive for Fijian musicians using stamping sticks (pages 4-5) and Aboriginal musician playing wooden clappers (page 6). Bate Collection for Indonesian saron (page 23). Clive Barda Performing Arts Library for orchestral gong (page 12); Evelyn Glennie (page 25) and orchestral tubular bells (page 37). Bridgeman Art Library for *Three Musicians and a Dancing Girl* (page 30), by courtesy of the Board of Trustees of the Victoria and Albert Museum and *Richard Wagner* by Gemalde von Schweninsky. The Trustees of the British Museum for Ancient Egyptian sistrum (page 8). Compix/Terry Short for thumb piano and gourd resonator from Zimbabwe (page 19). The Horniman Museum and Gardens for Ancient Egyptian hand clappers (page 6); South African mbira (page 18); gourd xylophone from Sierra Leone (page 22) and jingle from Spain (page 31). Hutchison Library for Tibetan group playing cymbals (page 10); kulintangan from the Philippines (page 13); khong wong lek from Thailand (page 13); mouth harp players from the Bing Gong orchestra in Bali (page 19); marimba band from Guatemala (page 23); gamelan orchestra from Bali (page 27); Indonesian puppet theatre (page 28); Tibetan monks playing hand bells (page 34) and musical saw player from New York (page 38). Redferns for modern drum set (page 11) and washboard player from an American skiffle band (page 17). Spectrum Colour Library for Russian Kolokol Bell (page 32) and Japanese temple bell (page 33).

The publishers would also like to give special thanks to Kate Davies, Mickleburgh Music Shop, Bristol, England and St. John the Baptist Church, Colerne, England for the loan of musical instruments.

DATE			